Time Management

A Comprehensive Manual That Presents You With
Cutting-edge Strategies And Methodologies For
Optimizing Your Tips

*(Enhancing Productivity And Achieving Success Via The
Implementation Of Efficient Time Management Strategies)*

Pascal Rauscher

TABLE OF CONTENT

Effective Time Management: Strategies For Efficient Time Allocation 1

Strategies For Educating Your Children On Time Management 9

How Motivation Impacts Focus 17

Recognize The Importance Of Setting Boundaries! 30

Leapfrogging Habits 52

What Are The Potential Benefits Of Implementing Time Management Practices In My Life? 101

Organizing Your Life 105

Optimal Timeframe For Addressing Routine Responsibilities 110

The Procrastination-Action Line 139

Effective Techniques For Time Management: Unveiling The Power Of Small And Large Strategies 154

Effective Time Management: Strategies For Efficient Time Allocation

Effective time management entails allocating a portion of one's day to accomplish a specific objective. The general consensus among individuals is that the available time in a single day is insufficient for accomplishing all the necessary tasks. This sensation is overpowering and can hinder our ability to accomplish the essential tasks on a daily basis or establish fresh objectives to strive for.

Allocating your time may appear effortless in theory, yet executing a comprehensive and efficient allocation is a contrasting matter.

Certain individuals may assert that allocating time each day is a straightforward undertaking that does not necessitate committing it to writing, as one can maintain the records mentally. It is a widely acknowledged fact that human beings frequently experience lapses in memory and often question why they did not make written records of important information.

I, too, previously pondered upon the query of effectively managing my time. I am well acquainted with the sensation of returning to one's dwelling after work and completing the routine errands, only to realize upon settling down that one inadvertently neglected visits to the financial institution or acquisition of dairy products.

The identical phenomenon occurs to your aspirations when they are not recorded and organized; they are easily disregarded and deprioritized.

An initial fundamental principle is to document all of your objectives and subsequently devise plans for their accomplishment. There exists a plethora of programs and applications presently accessible at no cost.

Strategies for Increasing Efficiency and Productivity

One of the primary obstacles individuals encounter in both their personal and professional lives pertains to the excessive workload relative to the limited timeframe available to accomplish tasks. Returning to the query at hand, what measures can one undertake to enhance productivity within a limited timeframe? The notion that attaining your objectives expeditiously does not necessarily equate to having extra leisure time.

Ranking Your Tasks

Have you ever experienced the situation where you commenced efforts on a particular task, yet found it challenging to maintain focus due to preoccupying thoughts about another task? This is quite prevalent. One potential factor contributing to being easily distracted is attributable to fear. Nevertheless, if we consider that your concern is not influencing your perspective, it would be advisable to commence evaluating the prioritization of your tasks.

It is worth noting that a significant number of individuals generate to-do lists; however, they often neglect the fundamental aspect of prioritizing the tasks listed. Alternatively, even if individuals give precedence to the task list, there are other tasks in another facet of their life that hold greater significance. Hence, it is exceedingly effortless for one to divert their attention towards alternative matters whilst engrossed in the completion of their assigned tasks.

Therefore, I would like to present you with the following instructions: Prioritize your tasks according to their level of importance.

Clearly, one must begin by contemplating the various obligations one has in their life. If you are similar to the majority of individuals, you likely possess numerous obligations and responsibilities encompassing family, employment, personal connections, domestic duties, and so forth.

Initially, enumerate the obligations you possess within the distinct categories mentioned earlier. Subsequently, prioritize these obligations based on their significance. For instance, in the event that your family relies upon your financial contributions, then your professional obligations may take priority. That implies you will uphold your professional obligations unless an unforeseen circumstance arises.

Furthermore, establish a series of task lists corresponding to each of your obligations. If you are employed in an external occupation, it is advisable to maintain your task agenda within the confines of your workplace. In the domestic setting, the list of tasks to be accomplished within your household typically comprises activities such as grocery shopping, arranging appointments with the dentist for children, and engaging in cleaning routines, among others. Ultimately, it is recommended to establish daily and weekly task lists that are aligned with your set objectives.

Please proceed to prioritize all of your tasks according to their respective levels of importance. The items positioned at the top of the list should be regarded as your utmost priorities, and it is strongly advised that these are the items you attend to personally. Nevertheless, please attempt to delegate or outsource the tasks that are of lesser priority on your agenda.

The main point to consider is that it is advisable to prioritize the significant tasks in your life and delegate the less important tasks to another individual. By doing so, you will have more time available to dedicate greater care and attention to the tasks of importance.

You have the ability to record all of your dreams, ideas, and goals in a single, centralized location. Furthermore, it is possible to monitor and document your progress, augmenting visual aids such as photographs to enhance your visualization and attainment of your objectives.

Furthermore, it offers a time allocation feature which facilitates the calculation of one's daily schedule, allowing for the division of time into necessary segments to ensure adequate time is allotted for completing essential tasks.

Strategies For Educating Your Children On Time Management

It is commonly acknowledged that prior to the commencement of the academic year, it is necessary for us to arrange regular medical checkups and engage in back-to-school purchasing. However, what measures can we adopt to establish a foundation for our children's achievements that will endure not only throughout the academic year but also in the long run? Through the act of granting our children the ability to effectively manage their time.

Set a bedtime.

Gradually reintegrate your children into a regular sleep regimen a week or two prior to the commencement of the school term. Children between the ages of 5 and 12 require approximately 10 to 11 hours of sleep on a daily basis.

Establish a suitable time for retiring to bed and adhere to it consistently.

Transform your child's daily regimen into a comprehensive list of tasks to be accomplished.

Engaging in this particular activity is the most effective measure one can undertake to alleviate familial stress in the course of the week. Throughout the academic year, children typically adhere to a consistent daily regimen, involving activities such as dressing and bathing. Rather than persistently pestering your children to complete tasks, it is advisable to collaborate with them by devising a customized checklist encompassing personal care responsibilities and age-appropriate household chores. Ensure they are held responsible for completing their assignments. When individuals express their lack of knowledge by saying "but I didn't know!" or seek guidance by asking "what should I do now?", kindly direct them to refer to the provided chart. No more excuses.

Facilitate the children in crafting personalized calendars.

Collaborate with your children to incorporate extracurricular activities into a digital or tangible schedule, aiding their understanding of their daily routine and facilitating their adjustment to the academic environment. The sooner your children commence acquiring knowledge in calendaring, the more self-reliant they shall become, thereby reducing the amount of assistance you need to provide for them (which is advantageous!).

Utilize time to their advantage.

Although it is likely that your children possess the ability to read analog clocks, they might not fully comprehend the significance of this skill. Aid them in cultivating a heightened mindfulness of time by purchasing a timepiece and instructing them in the art of accurately estimating the duration required to accomplish regular duties.

Teach kids to plan.

Ensuring punctuality and preparedness necessitates strategic arrangement. Is it necessary for your child to bring their homework or submit a permission slip? Does she need sports gear for after school? At what time should your child commence their preparations to ensure our timely departure? Publish a comprehensive list encompassing the tasks that individuals ought to undertake, along with the designated timings for their completion, thus ensuring everyone's responsibility in adhering to the planned departure time.

Establish set meal times.

Establishing fixed meal schedules for the entire family, such as having breakfast at 7 a.m., not only fosters time consciousness in your children but also guarantees valuable family moments.

Enact regulations pertaining to the use of electronic devices (farewell, iPad at bedtime!).

It is widely acknowledged that it is detrimental to remain fixated on screens continuously throughout the day. Numerous parents institute the parameters of "what, when, and how much" pertaining to screen time, yet it is equally advisable to establish a definite designated period for technology usage cessation, whereby all screens are switched off for the duration of the night. Yes, parents, too.

Designate a study zone.

Children require a dedicated study space wherein they can engage in their academic tasks devoid of any disturbances. Have you devised a strategy for organizing the documents that are brought home from school? Certain items must be retained, while others may be disposed of in the recycling bin. Determine the methodology by which you will effectively administer the circulation of documents.

Allow your children to express their concerns.

Provide your children with the chance to express any apprehensions they may have regarding resuming their education. The introduction of new teacher expectations, regulations, or a different educational institution can potentially induce feelings of anxiety. After the individuals have expressed their concerns, engage in a collective process of generating solutions through collaborative thinking. The implementation of a well-defined strategy can alleviate anxiety and facilitate a seamless transition for all parties involved.

Adopt the role of a mentor, rather than that of a supervisor.

With the onset of the academic year, there arises an increment in obligations and a surge in possibilities for discord between parents and their children. Contemplate adopting a cognitive transformation, transitioning from the role of your children's manager to that of their coach. In the capacity of a manager, you consistently remind your children to complete tasks due to a sense of accountability for the end result. That is the moment at which individuals firmly establish their position and the ensuing conflict for control commences. In the role of a coach, you assume the role of a compassionate external entity offering direction and encouragement. You equip your children with knowledge and then refrain from intervening, enabling them to exercise independent decision-making, be it beneficial or detrimental. It proves to be a source of liberation for all individuals, effectively fostering lasting self-assurance in children.

How Motivation Impacts Focus

Although goal setting is an effective approach to efficiently accomplish tasks and enhance their feasibility, its realization is futile in the absence of intrinsic motivation. Motivation can be deficient due to various factors, yet discovering means to augment workplace motivation coincides with enhancing one's concentration abilities. Enhancing one's performance via self-motivation is a notable and widely recognized characteristic observed in a significant proportion of accomplished business professionals across the globe. However, the methodology employed by these individuals to achieve this outcome remains a subject of inquiry. Let us examine the influence of motivation on concentration and achievement, and subsequently explore the strategies employed by influential global figures to harness the power of motivation.

What is Motivation?

Prior to delving into the examination of how motivation influences one's capacity to concentrate on and attain objectives, it is imperative to establish a comprehensive comprehension of the essence and nature of motivation. In its most rudimentary essence, motivation serves as the impetus for our triumphs, propelling us towards the pursuit of accomplishment. Lack of motivation often leads to a disregarding attitude towards achieving goals, to the extent that we may not even establish any goals in the first place. Moreover, when motivation is absent, our ability to concentrate diminishes, and consequently, our chances of achieving success diminish as well. Consider this: Can you recall any instances where the CEO of a prominent corporation achieved prosperity despite showing a lack of concern for their organization, its accomplishments, or its public perception? Rarely does it happen. Why? Since these CEOs are driven by their commitment to these factors, attributed to the fact that their achievements are intrinsically bound to the prosperity of their respective companies.

The Correlation Between Motivation and Concentration "The Relationship Between Motivation and Attention "The Linkage Between Motivation and Cognitive Focus

The connection between motivation and focus is mutually reinforcing. In the absence of sufficient motivation, it is highly improbable that we will direct our attention towards a given task. Indeed, as human beings, we inherently require a sense of purpose in order to undertake actions. This purpose can take the form of anticipated monetary gains or the satisfaction derived from accomplishing a task. Without this intrinsic motivator, our ability to concentrate on achieving success becomes significantly diminished. On the contrary, if we fail to allocate sufficient attention to a task, our motivation to finish it is likely to diminish. For instance, when confronted with a task that has languished on the outskirts of our desk for several months, our inclination to complete said task is unlikely to be high since, ultimately, its duration of wait has already been quite substantial. Through the omission of a specified deadline for the task's fulfillment or the establishment of incremental objectives to guide its attainment, we deprive ourselves of the necessary impetus to channel our efforts towards decisive action.

Implement Motivating Apps

In a similar vein, apps can function as a highly effective means to establish, monitor, and evaluate progress in the pursuit of goals, while simultaneously exerting a significant impact on enhancing motivation. There exists a multitude of motivational applications available for trial, however, we have compiled a selection of our preferred choices.

1. BeeMinder introduces an additional element to the notion of incentivization. This complimentary application strives to foster the accomplishment of objectives and assignments, by encouraging users to establish goals and place a tangible monetary wager on their capability to achieve these objectives. Presently, individuals will not receive financial compensation upon achieving their objectives; however, there is an obligation to incur payment in the event of non-compliance. Is there a superior methodology for incentivizing individuals to undertake meaningful advancements than compelling them to bear financial consequences for their inaction?

2. Unstuck – An additional complimentary application, Unstuck has been developed to assist individuals in overcoming periods of stagnation. This

app places emphasis on fostering your motivation through the means of peer and digital mentorship, as well as effective problem-solving strategies.

3. Happier, a complimentary application centered on enhancing happiness levels, is designed to serve as a source of inspiration and motivation. The purpose of Happier is to encourage individuals to accumulate and acknowledge a series of positive experiences throughout the day, which can subsequently serve as a source of inspiration and contribute to enhancing their overall emotional well-being. A favorable mindset plays a significant role in stimulating us to attain our objectives, even if they appear unattainable.

4. Headout is an application that is centered around the notion of experiential motivation, and it is available free of charge. We have previously addressed the significance of

occasionally taking a break from work, and Headout effectively capitalizes on this notion. By enumerating nearby events and locations that you can visit, this application provides you with inspiration for taking a break, thus allowing you to return with revitalized determination to achieve your objectives.

Alternative Strategies for Enhancing Motivation

Applications serve as an excellent initial resource for enhancing one's level of motivation. It is imperative to acknowledge, nevertheless, that on certain occasions, in order to enhance our motivation, we must also enact modifications to our lifestyles. These alterations may present challenges or prove to be straightforward; nevertheless, one can be assured that undertaking any of them will amplify one's motivation and augment one's concentration on achieving success.

Practice Positivity

Our level of motivation in life is greatly influenced by our perspective on things. Should we persist in perceiving the world with a pessimistic perspective, our attention will invariably be directed towards the unfavorable aspects, consequently impeding our efforts to undertake meaningful endeavors. Counteract this negativity by embracing positivity in all aspects of your daily routine. Discovering a positive aspect in every endeavor undertaken prompts an enhanced drive, promoting diligence, objectives attainment, and ultimately, triumph.

Utilize Visualization

The act of mentally picturing our achievement serves as an ideal method to direct our concentration towards the reasons behind our diligent efforts. Set aside a short period of time each day to engage in visualization exercises where you envisage yourself successfully attaining the goals you are actively working towards. What does your current life situation entail? How do you wish to proceed? Take pleasure in the feeling of contentment that you will experience and utilize this sentiment to drive your progress in accomplishing your objective.

Try Resetting

At some juncture, every individual experiences a loss of concentration. We succumb to the overwhelming preoccupations of daily life, leading to a sense of disorientation, which in turn dampens our drive. If you encounter this kind of situation, it is advisable to separate yourself from your workstation. Engage in a leisurely stroll amidst the woodland, discover a tranquil spot conducive to reading a literary work, embark upon an exploration of uncharted terrain within your local vicinity... undertake an activity that serves to recalibrate your mental state. Remove yourself from the intricate web of confusion and devote your attention solely to unwinding and revitalizing your inherent zest for life.

Release Your Fears

Frequently, individuals develop a fear of attaining success due to various factors, leading them to engage in self-sabotaging behavior. Our motivation diminishes as a result of this fear, and we endeavor to persuade ourselves that circumstances are truly acceptable as they currently stand. Instead of subjecting oneself to a self-constricting lifestyle, it is advisable to explore the concept of relinquishing control. Let go of your fears and recognize that they are merely constraining your abilities. Harness your desire for liberation from fear as your impetus towards triumph. Embrace the need for personal transformation and refuse to let fear impose limitations on your journey to success any further.

Recognize The Importance Of Setting Boundaries!

Mastering this principle can prove to be one of the most challenging endeavors. Determining the appropriate moment to decline can be challenging, as the act of refusal often engenders a multitude of diverse consequences. It is conceivable that a dear companion or family member may have a request or desire for your assistance, or that an acquaintance has extended an invitation for your participation in an enjoyable endeavor. While it may be your intention to demonstrate affection towards your loved one or seek enjoyment with your friend, there are occasions when it becomes necessary to decline. It is important to acknowledge that the constraints of time limit our availability, with a mere 24 hours allotted in a day, 7 days in a week, and 365 days in a year. You need to make the decision that enables you to utilize that time effectively.

This principle undoubtedly holds significant value among the 8 principles expounded upon in this book. Frequently, these unsolicited offers from acquaintances and relatives are presented abruptly and fail to align with our preexisting schedule. By affirming our agreement, we are essentially acknowledging our willingness to postpone our planned activities and indirectly suggesting that this newfound task holds greater significance. It is conceivable that a component of your daily regimen entailed waking up, engaging in physical exercise, and procuring sustenance for the subsequent week. By procrastinating on exercise and meal preparation, we might unknowingly be deferring more than we realize.

This meal preparation session will need to be allocated to a different day. Every instance in which we veer away from our predetermined daily schedule serves to augment our roster of pending tasks, thereby further lengthening the agenda for the subsequent day. This leads me to my subsequent guiding principle... PROCRASTINATION.

~ DON'T PROCRASTINATE ~

What is the definition of procrastination and what are some strategies to prevent it? Procrastination entails the habitual deferral of pressing matters in favor of less significant tasks, or the deliberate postponement or neglect of the task at hand. It has come to my attention that the perceived cause of numerous failures lies in the act of procrastination.

Delays can manifest themselves in various ways. Certain individuals engage in the act of procrastination by prioritizing simpler tasks over more challenging ones. Many individuals opt to disregard the fact that certain tasks require attention and instead choose to engage in a state of inaction.

By adhering to my additional 12 suggestions, you will be able to prevent procrastination as they demand strict adherence to the following guidelines:

- Clearly delineate your objectives and ascertain the purpose behind each task.
- Develop a comprehensive strategy and diligently execute it! (Neglecting to strategize is preparing for failure)
- Generate a task inventory sorted based on priority
- Divide the extensive tasks into several smaller ones
- Inform others of your intentions so that they may hold you accountable.

- Establish an incentive system with corresponding consequences for the more challenging tasks.
- Be aware that there will perpetually remain tasks to be completed.
- Do not hesitate to seek assistance. - Feel free to request support. - Please do not hesitate to reach out for help. - Do not fear approaching others for assistance.

~ FOCUS ~

In contemporary society, it is quite effortless to veer from recognizing the fundamental aspects of significance. We allocate our time to engaging in social media platforms and extensive internet browsing, ultimately resulting in time consumption. We have experienced a decline in our ability to engage in social interactions and now allocate a significant portion of our time with loved ones to staring at handheld devices. This is a practice that is not embraced by individuals who have achieved success.

In truth, the majority of accomplished individuals utilize social media as a means to enhance their achievements, without squandering their time perusing the social activities of former schoolmates or engaging in the narratives of others sharing grievances about their lives. Individuals who achieve success maintain a steadfast and unwavering concentration on the present assignment. In social settings, individuals engage in face-to-face interactions rather than opting for the online avenue of sharing a status update. Maintaining focus is a fundamental principle that often proves to be remarkably susceptible to deviation. When engaging in activities with friends and family, dedicate attention towards fostering the development of those relationships. While engaged in a specific assignment, it is advisable to refrain from frequent email checks and direct your concentration towards achieving timely completion of that task. When compiling your daily task agenda by analyzing the 'What?' and 'Why?' behind each item... In what manner could such urgency have been instilled or a compelling motive provided to ensure that one does not deviate from that objective? Please remain attentive and strive to obtain additional outcomes promptly.

Enhances Well-being and Mitigates Anxiety

To be completely forthright, a lack of medical or scientific evidence exists to substantiate the claim that planners enhance one's health. However, considering the matter from an alternate standpoint, a planner aids in the documentation of both personal and professional commitments. This implies that you have the ability to monitor and strategize your exercise sessions, regular walks, and any other health-related objectives. Interestingly, by ensuring that you do not miss a single dental appointment, you will effectively contribute to achieving your health objectives. Since that is the function of the planner, it serves as a reminder to maintain good health. Additionally, we experience anxiety in response to any form of uncertainty that arises in our existence. It instigates feelings of unease and imparts various health-related complications. A planner allows individuals to effectively generate and oversee various activities within a single consolidated medium. Upon awakening each morning and perceiving the presence of pending responsibilities, any apprehensions pertaining to ennui are dispelled, thereby channeling one's attention towards the completion of said tasks.

Evidence of Accomplishment

We all aspire to view ourselves as the complete embodiment of our potential, yet we must exercise patience until that defining culmination arrives. We are constantly evolving and improving, which presents us with a tremendous opportunity for growth. Nevertheless, a planner serves as a physical resource that documents one's previous achievements, serving as substantiation of one's diligent efforts. Upon reflecting and perusing through those pages, you will experience a profound sense of pride and a genuine feeling of achievement as you observe the remarkable progress you have made from your past state to your current one. It is an infectious sensation to experience. It serves as a powerful incentive to continually aspire for greater achievements and propels one's endeavors towards self-improvement. Regard a planner not merely as a tool for enhancing productivity, but rather as concrete testament to your diligent efforts and unwavering commitment. Although the challenge may appear overwhelming at this juncture, maintain a positive perspective as this marks the beginning of your journey. Since one can only progress from the current point and perceive greater opportunities for accomplishing significant feats.

Utilizing an Organizer for Enhanced Time Management.

When presented with a limited timeframe of 24 hours per day, it is essential to devise a strategic plan in order to maximize their utilization. One ought to consider their work responsibilities, daily household tasks, parental responsibilities if applicable, personal undertakings, physical fitness regimen, culinary pursuits, and recreational activities. There exists a multitude of tasks that can be accomplished during a single day, yet the constraint of time restricts this allocation to a mere 24 hours. On average, individuals are awake for no less than fifty percent of those hours, engaging in tasks of productivity. Therefore, for the purpose of this discussion, let us consider an average timeframe of 12 to 16 hours during which one can engage in meaningful activities. A scheduler will diligently manage and prompt you to complete tasks at the designated time. Nevertheless, it is essential to bear in mind that you remain the one responsible for making that choice. Therefore, it is essential to possess proficient time management abilities in order to effectively arrange your tasks within a planner. A planner primarily serves as a means of organizing and maintaining plans within its pages. It does not inherently constitute those plans. It is within the purview of your imaginative faculties to generate these ideas. I will furnish you with a set of strategies that you may employ when utilizing a planner with the intention of enhancing your temporal efficiency.

The Daily Highlight

The daily highlight is an intriguing methodology I acquired during the initial phases of my endeavor towards enhanced productivity. Upon extensive consumption of various literary works and online resources, this particular phenomenon emerged as prominently noteworthy. This aspect highlights the inherent beauty of the daily occurrence. It accentuates the core elements of utmost significance. Whenever I found myself beset by the demands of my planner, as I am confident you will experience in due course, the daily highlight proved to be an invaluable aid. Suppose you are confronted with approximately ten imperative tasks that necessitate completion within the course of the day; however, you must designate a solitary task, one that is non-negotiable and will unequivocally be accomplished by day's end, regardless of any unforeseen circumstances. No justifications can be made for this. It is imperative that you complete that particular task. In the event that you possess a roster of duties comprising a minimum of 5 to 10 tasks to be accomplished within a given day, it is imperative to prioritize the composition of a memorandum as the foremost and time-sensitive responsibility, thus ensuring its completion. An advantage I discovered upon integrating the daily highlight into my routine (which I continue to practice till date) is that it enabled me to prioritize and accomplish that specific task at the earliest juncture of my day. That particular task proved to be of utmost significance in attaining ultimate satisfaction. Consequently, I ensured the task's prompt completion. Surprisingly, engaging in that particular task served as a catalyst for my subsequent productivity, as it instilled in me a heightened sense of motivation and the drive to accomplish additional objectives throughout the day.

One additional advantage of the daily highlight is that it fosters the development of a productive routine. Consider the hypothetical scenario where you are granted the opportunity to acquire one item daily. Now, you shall establish a customary practice and engage in it consistently for a duration of one year. Hence, it can be inferred that you have successfully completed 365 significant tasks within the span of a year, as you diligently ensured the completion of the daily highlight on a daily basis. That succinctly encapsulates a significant factor in fostering your development, despite the seemingly incremental nature of the advancements. As opposed to engaging in excessive productivity on a single day and subsequently exhausting oneself for the next four to five days, you ensured the completion of one significant task each day. Positive behaviors such as these foster personal growth and self-improvement. Leverage the daily highlight as a strategic tool by encircling a single task each day that will be accomplished without fail. Utilizing a planner during one's initial stages proves to be an efficacious approach in addressing procrastination. It proved highly advantageous for me.

Time Allocation and Time Segmentation

Prominent tactics such as time allotment and scheduling compartments are utilized by accomplished business figures such as Bill Gates and Elon Musk as a routine practice. When implementing the practice of time blocking, one would allocate their day into distinct segments of time. Assuming one begins their day upon awakening at approximately 7 am and concludes it by retiring around 11 pm, one has the option to partition the hours into distinct time intervals. Within each designated time interval, you will be assigned a particular task or activity to concentrate on solely, disregarding any other obligation or diversion. If your intended period for focused work, such as writing, researching, coding, and other related tasks, is scheduled between 9 to 11 am, it is advisable to reserve this designated timeframe exclusively for those activities. After the designated time has elapsed, you will evaluate whether the task has been carried out in its entirety. If there are any outstanding tasks, you may choose to either pursue their completion or address them on the subsequent day. The outcome is contingent upon both the inherent characteristics and the level of immediacy associated with the assignment.

In the context of time boxing, the aim is to optimize time utilization by imposing limitations on unproductive activities and allocating predetermined time frames to complete productive tasks. Engaging in recreational internet browsing is perceived as lacking in productivity during a normal day. As such, the utilization of the time boxing technique will enable you to confine the allocated time for the aforementioned undertaking as required. If you dedicate a mere five minutes to scrolling, you will solely utilize those five minutes. After completing it, you proceed to the next assignment. Similarly, this principle can be applied to your tasks that contribute to productivity. Utilize this method to effectively organize your time in your planner. When a designated time frame is imposed upon a particular task, the phenomena known as Parkinson's Law ensues, thus enhancing the likelihood of successfully accomplishing the task within the stipulated duration. In conclusion, the utilization of time blocks or time boxes can assist in prioritizing essential tasks and allocating more dedicated time towards them during periods of peak productivity. While you have the ability to limit unproductive activities to a minimum, thereby enhancing your efficiency and productivity.

Striving for Equilibrium in Life

A prevalent fallacy that I often notice when individuals utilize a planner is that they solely employ it for documenting their professional obligations. That is not the proper manner in which one should utilize a planner. Due to the fact that one's existence encompasses more than solely occupational endeavors. One must prioritize nurturing personal relationships, tending to the needs of loved ones, ensuring personal well-being, and engaging in enjoyable pursuits during moments of leisure. Given this consideration, ensure that you fully integrate your entire life into your planner. Incorporate both personal and professional tasks and activities, encompassing your personal aspirations as well. The utmost importance in your life lies in the pursuit of greater significance and equilibrium. It is essential to encounter diverse instances throughout one's life, and a planner plays a crucial role in facilitating the organization and separation of personal and professional aspirations.

Establish a monthly objective for achievement.

To add an element of intrigue, consider devising a miniature objective for every month. It can be anything. It pertains to either your personal growth or any matter pertaining to business. As an illustration, I intend to acquire proficiency in the French language. I am undertaking this as an invigorating endeavor, concurrently acquiring proficiency in a foreign language. This endeavor is yielding positive results and I am augmenting my personal growth by acquiring an additional proficiency. You have the option to engage in a comparable activity. Consider identifying a specific objective you wish to achieve within the upcoming month or, alternatively, set a baseline measurement to initiate the process of long-term growth. The objective must be attainable, integral to one's personal development, and deliver considerable value. If you anticipate that achieving the goal may require more than a month, endeavor to schedule it within the span of a month and commence action. One may extend the momentum or progress into the subsequent month and persevere in striving towards that objective.

Less is More

Additionally, I would like to address the potentially laborious task of meticulously jotting down one's daily activities when utilizing a planner. This repetitive task of daily writing in a planner has the potential to induce fatigue among individuals, or elicit feelings of squandered time as they engage in this practice. One potential approach that could be employed is to employ brevity by utilizing a limited number of words (maximum two or three) to succinctly convey your tasks or objectives. When engaging in concise bullet point writing comprising only a couple of words, it contributes to time efficiency. Consequently, you will not experience fatigue from using your planner regularly. It suffices to utilize a mere two or three words to succinctly elucidate your undertakings and intentions. Upon reflection, these plans will be remembered by you as they were documented by you.

Leapfrogging Habits

10. Observe your habits
11. Some individuals refer to this practice as habit stacking; however, what you are undertaking is the cultivation of novel habits that will significantly contribute to your overall productivity. Document the daily habits that you currently possess. This brings one's attention to actions that are often executed unconsciously or without deliberate consideration. For instance, how do you respond to the advent of morning or the sound of the alarm clock? What's your routine? Would you happen to visit the restroom beforehand? May I inquire if you possess a bathing facility? The objective is to pay attention to those actions that are performed

effortlessly and automatically, as I am going to demonstrate methods for cultivating positive routines that address the neglected aspects of your life.

12.

13. Leapfrogging habits

14. Integrate a fresh habit into one or two of your preexisting ones. Exercise caution in your level of ambition, as it is more advisable to establish a few habits successfully rather than attempting to excessively broaden your range of habits and ultimately experiencing failure. For instance, if you have a routine that you engage in during the evening hours, conclude it by composing a list of your goals for the upcoming day. In the morning, consider incorporating a 10-minute meditation session following your awakening. It aids in

eliminating mental clutter and enables one to approach the day with a optimistic mindset. If you tend to exhibit laziness in attending to household chores, consider incorporating them into your current routine. For instance, when utilizing the lavatory, incorporate the act of cleaning the lavatory into your established routine, ensuring it is performed consistently on every occasion.

15.
16. The benefits of cultivating habits lie in their ability to facilitate effortless achievement, leading to enhanced punctuality, improved efficiency, and heightened rates of success. Now consider your daily activities in the workplace. An excellent practice for enhancing productivity can be incorporated in the following manner:

17.
18. Introduce Peace
19. Upon your arrival at the workplace, commence a period of tranquility. This enables you to accomplish a significant amount and allocate your cognitive resources towards overcoming any challenges you may encounter throughout the day. During this time, it is appropriate to kindly request that your colleagues respect your need for privacy, silence your mobile devices, activate voicemail on your phone, and take the opportunity to carefully evaluate your tasks for the day. If you encounter challenging tasks, seize this opportunity to tackle them, for once the difficult tasks have been completed, it contributes to an overall perception of the day as being more manageable.
20.

21.
22. Learn to prioritize
23. Amidst moments of serenity, endeavor to establish priorities. This signifies the establishment of three distinct groups, wherein each encompasses the tasks that are pending and necessitate your attention every morning:
24.
25. Immediate attention required
26. • Somewhat pressing • Moderately urgent • Fairly time-sensitive • Relatively important
27. • Of little significance • Insignificant • Is of minimal importance • Lacks significance • Holds little weight • Carries low importance • Is of lesser consequence
28. This enables you to effectively structure your day

to ensure tasks are tackled in a sequential and prioritized manner. Please be mindful that discontinuing a task to address an interruption inevitably requires a period of time to regain your previous level of focus and productivity. Thus, engaging in multitasking is not conducive to achieving optimal outcomes. The human brain possesses the ability to effectively handle one task at a time; therefore, it is advisable to prioritize the activity that exhibits the highest level of importance, as less demanding tasks can be attended to later in the day.

29.

30. On a daily basis, you partake in the midday meal. You may choose to take a brief break for a meal and continue working simultaneously; however, I would like to elaborate on why this practice is insufficient for

maintaining punctuality and inhibits your progress. Consuming a brief refreshment fails to afford you the necessary respite from your work obligations. Taking this break rejuvenates you, enabling you to generate a moment of heightened energy upon your return from lunch. Therefore, utilize this subsequent piece of guidance during your post-lunch period characterized by heightened energy levels.

31.
32. Learn to delegate
33. At this juncture, it is expected that you possess an understanding of the tasks that require attention and their corresponding levels of urgency. Nevertheless, in the event that someone demonstrates a superior performance, utilize this post-

lunch interval to assign tasks to the staff member who excels in the respective area. This does not indicate any shortcomings in your abilities. Indeed, this possibility does exist; however, assigning tasks to others enables you to effectively oversee personnel and maintain harmonious relationships with your fellow workers. Therefore, if you are able to cultivate this habit, you may potentially be on track towards advancement within your career. Cease monopolizing all of your own tasks. By placing your trust in others and delegating tasks that align with their skills, you can cultivate stronger interpersonal relationships and elicit a willingness for them to assist you in subsequent occasions.

34.

35. Please bear in mind that in cases where an existing habit is present, it would be advantageous to incorporate an additional one. Over time, you will discover that it will facilitate your progress in productivity and enhance your ability to effectively manage time.
36.
37. Handle all emails or client communication in one consolidated effort.
38. In this manner, incessant interruptions resulting from client phone calls and emails are minimized. You will no longer need to constantly monitor your inbox for pending emails, as you will have configured an automated response system. This practice enables you to significantly save time. Consequently, during the time slot designated

for addressing customer inquiries, you can allocate uninterrupted attention and promptly respond to each query, effectively clearing your email account. Please ensure to assign those tasks to individuals who are better equipped to handle them. Upon completion, kindly deactivate your email account and abstain from reviewing it until your upcoming designated email session. By incorporating various habits into your routine and consistently practicing them, you will eventually internalize them, performing them effortlessly and without conscious effort.

39.
40. Develop, organize, implement
41. Every prosperous entrepreneur adheres to a

single practice in order to maintain concentration and organization throughout their day: each one follows a prescribed work regimen.

42. In the event that you are faced with an abundant amount of tasks, you may experience a sense of overwhelm, making it increasingly challenging to initiate your work. Establishing a regular schedule will provide the necessary framework to efficiently accomplish a significant amount of work within a limited timeframe.

43. The crux lies in organizing your priorities rather than giving precedence to your schedule.

44. Typically, approximately 40 percent of one's working hours are devoted to non-productive activities. By establishing a

structured schedule and implementing effective techniques, one can efficiently manage their day and substantially enhance productivity.

45. Below, you will find several pointers that can assist you in enhancing your time management abilities and overall productivity.

46. Take a Break

47. It is impossible for individuals to maintain productivity consistently throughout the entire duration of a day. It is crucial to incorporate periodic intervals of respite throughout the day to allow for cognitive rejuvenation. Engaging in this activity will afford you the opportunity to rejuvenate and enhance your productivity.

48. To ensure survival and optimal well-being, it is

imperative to incorporate periodic intervals of repose and engagement. Mental resilience, engagement, and aptitude will fluctuate, thus necessitating appropriate preparation and adaptation.

49. Consolidate Tasks with Similar Characteristics
50. There exists a subset of individuals who posit their adeptness in managing multiple tasks simultaneously, yet this assertion remains largely fallacious. Engaging in multitasking beyond two simultaneous tasks will result in a reduction of productivity by approximately 40 percent. However, I do possess a companion with whom I have engaged in telephonic conversations whilst concurrently composing a blog entry. This is highly commendable given that multitasking typically

compromises the integrity of one's work. As the human brain alternates between tasks, our focus likewise shifts, leading to a divided attention that fails to allocate full commitment to any given task. Instead of attempting to simultaneously complete multiple tasks, it is advisable to categorize similar tasks and address them in consolidated periods. This could entail confining all telephone communications to a designated hour or generating content during a specific period.

51. Time blocking refers to a proactive approach of prearranging and allocating specific time slots throughout the day for accomplishing designated tasks, thus establishing clear timelines for their completion. Once you have acquired this information,

kindly ensure to schedule these tasks in your calendar and subsequently allocate time during the optimal period, specifically midday, for their completion. Implementing time blocking techniques allows for enhanced focus on individual tasks, thereby heightening productivity throughout the course of the day.

52. When engaging in organizational activities, ensure that you allocate dedicated time for both reactive and proactive tasks. Reactive blocks encompass the periods during which one accommodates interruptions and external demands, such as attending to emergency meetings and responding to emails. During proactive blocks, your attention will be devoted to accomplishing the critical tasks on your agenda.

At this stage, you will commence the process of outlining the prototype for your upcoming project and composing critical documents or essential undertakings.

53. It could be advantageous to prioritize the most demanding task during the initial hours of the day and subsequently dedicate the latter part of the day to reviewing your email correspondence. This maintains focus and ensures that phone calls and emails can be addressed at a later time.

54. This approach affords you the benefit of precise time allocation and a clear understanding of when you will complete your tasks. Basic task lists merely serve as a documentation of the tasks that necessitate completion. Time blocking entails generating a comprehensive task inventory alongside

predetermined time slots for their execution.

55. By imposing a strict framework upon yourself and obligating yourself to complete your tasks within the allotted time frame, you are compelling yourself to maintain a concentrated focus on all of your responsibilities. Developing a premeditated schedule on a calendar will facilitate the maintenance of concentration on paramount tasks. Regardless of one's perspective, it is an undeniable fact that tasks require a certain amount of time to be completed.

56. Focus Sessions

57. Engaging in constant task switching may give the illusion of busyness, yet it does not yield substantial productivity. One should prioritize productivity by allocating a

dedicated time slot to concentrate solely on the most significant task at hand.

58. Human cognition operates within finite constraints, thereby necessitating the optimal utilization of our limited periods of deep concentration for utmost critical analysis. Optimal efficiency and output are achieved through continuous ninety-minute intervals; therefore, it is advisable to structure your schedule into segments of ninety minutes. During each of these designated time intervals, refrain from engaging in any other tasks and maintain distance from any sources of distraction. Kindly inform your colleagues that you will be occupied during this period and politely request them to refrain from disturbing you. In this manner, you will be able to

maintain your concentration undisturbed.

59. Our physiological systems function in accordance with ultradian rhythms. These cycles exhibit zeniths when we experience the highest levels of energy, succeeded by a phase of greater fatigue. Through the utilization of ninety-minute sessions, you can effectively harness the bursts of energy that occur throughout the day. You will engage in a period of work lasting ninety minutes, followed by a designated interval of rest ranging from twenty to thirty minutes. The intermission between work sessions is crucial for enhancing performance.

60. A considerable number of individuals tend to disregard the innate rhythms of their bodies, resorting to stimulants such as coffee in order to effectively navigate their daily

obligations. Typically, this results in a total system failure around 2:30 p.m.

61. By adopting a pattern of working in ninety-minute intervals, you can effectively optimize your energy levels for completing necessary tasks and significantly enhance your overall productivity. Rather than opposing your body, you will be cooperating with it.

62. Our mindset has been shaped by the practice of consistently adhering to an eight-hour work day, leading us to believe that we must maintain a continuous work schedule starting from eight o'clock in the morning until five in the evening. You are only granted a respite during the midday mealtime, allowing you to maintain your peak performance throughout the entirety of your workday. While this aids in maintaining

managerial oversight over employees, it will adversely impact productivity.

63. There are disadvantages associated with this particular system. It is advisable to avoid being discovered by your employer while reclining on the floor of your workspace, napping. They may not experience contentment, despite being informed of your alignment with your innate biological patterns and the assistance provided to enhance your cognitive recall. You may encounter time constraints that necessitate continuous work efforts.

64. When carefully planning your schedule and avoiding time constraints, consider aligning your activities with the natural rhythm of your body. It is conceivable that your bodily functions may not operate according to ninety-

minute intervals; however, it is advisable to observe and assess your inherent energy patterns over a span of several weeks in order to establish an optimal routine.

65. Eat the Frog
66. You are not going to engage in the physical act of consuming a frog. This pertains to the task that you have an aversion to, yet are undeniably obliged to undertake. You may be deterred from engaging in the activity due to its inherent unpleasantness or the potential challenges it presents. The majority of individuals will exert all efforts to avoid engaging in activities that they find unpleasant. The act of appearing preoccupied serves as a façade to circumvent essential yet discomforting responsibilities. By prioritizing "eating the

frog" as the first task in the morning, rather than allowing it to be a source of worry throughout the day, one can experience increased productivity and a smoother day overall. You will experience a sense of relief as if a burden has been lifted off your shoulders. Additionally, you will experience a sense of accomplishment, and you can now remove that arduous task from your list.

67. Direct your attention towards merely three tasks on a daily basis.
68. This strategy is commonly referred to as the "most significant task approach." It involves directing one's attention towards matters of utmost importance. An alternative approach would involve prioritizing the three most crucial tasks and dedicating focused efforts

towards their completion, as opposed to compiling an extensive list of tasks and attempting to tackle them all simultaneously. There are additional tasks that you are capable of undertaking, however, it is not necessary for you to concern yourself with any other matters until completion of those three tasks has been attained.

69. Typically, there are only a few tasks that require completion on a regular basis. You may encounter a multitude of voices vying for your attention; however, it should be noted that these voices hold no significance. The numerous notifications in your electronic correspondences and mobile device can all be deferred. By successfully completing those three paramount tasks, all

other endeavors will become superfluous.

70. Once you have determined the top three prioritized tasks, proceed to allocate them to the initial segment of your day. You will have the opportunity to accomplish some headway on the critical tasks before encountering the various disturbances. This can be employed in conjunction with time blocking, should you wish to do so, however, it is advised to allocate the initial few hours for prioritized tasks. The completion of your tasks should take priority over attending meetings, engaging in phone calls, or responding to emails. When you can focus on these tasks, your days will become more constructive. You shall never experience a day in which you squander your time on futile endeavors.

71. Engaging in a perpetual cycle of attending to minor tasks and resolving immediate problems will impede your ability to focus on realizing larger objectives. This task can be accomplished either the evening prior or as a first priority each morning. Organize your timetable in accordance with these tasks and eliminate any potential distractions.

72. If you allocate the time frame from 9 to 11 to solely focus on your initial task, it is advisable to disable social media, email notifications, and refrain from engaging with your phone. In the event that your workplace lacks a door, you may opt to utilize a set of noise-canceling headphones. Additionally, you may consider opting for a more tranquil environment such as a library or a coffee shop.

73. It can be effortless to become entangled in the monotonous routine of everyday life; nevertheless, it is imperative to constantly bear in mind your ultimate objectives. Maintaining focus by minimizing distractions and refraining from interruptions can significantly enhance productivity. A significant proportion of the workforce dedicates approximately two hours per day towards recuperating from various interruptions.
74. Plan Your Day
75. On average, employees allocate approximately thirteen hours per week to respond to email correspondence. If you check your email at the beginning of the day, it will take up all your time. When there are alternative activities available to engage in. A significant

portion of individuals allocate excessive amounts of time to matters of urgency while neglecting activities that hold substantial importance. Prior to accessing your email, allocate a moment to record your daily tasks and objectives. You may compile this list towards the conclusion of the day in order to prepare for the following day. This facilitates the completion of a greater quantity of tasks and ensures that the work being performed is optimized for business enhancement.

76. Morning Ritual
77. Each individual's morning routine will vary. "Allow me to present the morning routines of several highly accomplished individuals:
78. Tony Robbins: He does not adhere to a designated waking time. Upon rising, he promptly

immerses himself either in a cryotherapy tank or the pool. Subsequently, he will engage in meditation and consume a breakfast that is rich in protein.

79. Richard Branson: He rises at the early hour of five each morning. He engages in cardiovascular activities such as running or playing tennis, and partakes in breakfast alongside his family. Subsequently, he will peruse the news articles and verify his electronic mail.

80. Arianna Huffington: She abstains from utilizing an alarm clock. She refrains from inspecting her phone until she has engaged in a brief meditation session.

81. Oprah Winfrey: Upon rising, she engages in oral hygiene practices, takes her dog for a stroll, engages in physical

exercise, partakes in moments of deep introspection, consumes her morning meal, and reviews her daily agenda.

82. Mark Zuckerberg: He does not rise at an early hour. After awakening, he will proceed to engage in either physical exercise or go for a jog, partake in breakfast, dress himself appropriately, and then depart for the premises of Facebook headquarters.

83. Elon Musk begins his day by dedicating thirty minutes to the perusal of significant emails, after which he proceeds to indulge in a cup of coffee, takes a refreshing shower, and subsequently arrives at his place of work.

84. Creating Your Routine

85. It is evident that individuals do not possess identical daily schedules. It pertains to commencing your day in a

manner that aligns with your individual preferences and needs. If you aspire to establish a morning routine, allow me to propose a few notions that may serve as a launching pad for your endeavor:

86. Allocate time for activities that bring you joy and satisfaction, such as engaging in a hobby, taking leisurely strolls with your canine companion, or indulging in a nourishing breakfast. It will provide a valuable context and elevate your mood.

87. Please review your calendar: By doing so, you will have a clear understanding of what to anticipate throughout the day. It ensures that potential conflicts can be addressed proactively, mitigating the risk of untimely resolution.

88. Establish daily objectives: Articulating your goals increases the likelihood of achieving them by 50 percent. You will experience an enhanced sense of autonomy and agency in managing your life.

89. Adhere to a nutritious diet, engage in mindfulness practices, and engage in physical activity. One might assume that it is generally understood by the majority that remaining in bed and consuming doughnuts will not provide one with the necessary vitality to successfully navigate one's daily activities.

90. Rise earlier than your companions: This will provide you with an opportunity to engage in meditation, strategize for the day ahead, engage in writing or reading, or attend to your electronic

correspondence, all devoid of any interruptions.

91. Avoid working during the midday hours.

92. The individuals who are highly efficient in their work will strategically organize their timetables in accordance with their peak productivity hours. Consequently, if you possess a propensity for staying awake during nocturnal hours, waking up early would prove to be counterproductive. Due to the fact that the majority of individuals exhibit high levels of productivity in the morning, particularly within the few hours after awakening, it would be advisable to refrain from engaging in work activities during the midday period.

93. Engaging in physical activity is highly beneficial for enhancing energy levels and

augmenting productivity. Nonetheless, it is important to recognize that concentration and vitality inherently fluctuate throughout the course of the day. If your primary objective is optimizing your initial priorities, engaging in gym activities would necessitate a compromise of your valuable time dedicated to productivity. You may consider commencing your activities during the late afternoon or mid-morning. Commencing your departure from the workplace in the midst of the day may evoke a sense of strangeness, yet it could serve as a means of curbing the frequency of breaks taken throughout the day, and potentially reduce your dependence on excessive coffee consumption.

Arrange Meetings and Telephone Conversations during the Afternoon

Due to the innate circadian rhythm present in every individual, a phenomenon known as cognitive haze is commonly observed during the afternoon hours. Instead of attempting to resist it, consider taking a brief rest or enjoying a small refreshment. This may serve as a source of inspiration, encouraging you to persevere throughout the remainder of your day.

Due to a decrease in your energy levels during the afternoon, it would be advisable for you to allocate your productive hours to more demanding and innovative tasks. This indicates that your responsibilities solely entail engaging in tasks of a non-demanding nature, such as attending meetings or responding to phone calls. There is a growing recognition among individuals that holding meetings at three o'clock in the afternoon is highly advantageous.

The 52/17 Principle

We are not robots. It is imperative that we allocate periods of respite throughout the day to maintain a state of alertness and ensure optimal productivity. This is the reason why a multitude of individuals are adopting the Pomodoro Technique, a method that advocates for the completion of tasks through brief, concentrated and efficient work periods, followed by a brief intermission. A timer is the only necessary tool for this. It provides you with the opportunity to divide large tasks into smaller, more feasible segments.

This is the procedure:

Select a task to undertake

Establish a timer for a duration of 25 minutes.

Please continue with your household duties until the timer signals the completion period.

Please pause your work for a brief period of five minutes.

During each session, your break duration will progressively increase.

This will enable you to enhance your daily productivity while still incorporating periods of rest. These abbreviated sessions afford you the opportunity to concentrate without succumbing to cognitive exhaustion.

After conducting a thorough analysis of employee behavior, Desktop has discovered that the average productivity level amounts to a working period of 52 minutes, followed by a rest period of 17 minutes. Notwithstanding the precise duration of your work sessions, it is imperative to recognize the importance of taking periodic breaks to realign your focus, reenergize yourself, and prevent exhaustion-induced decline.

Notwithstanding its apparent simplicity, this technique does possess a drawback. These sessions are not intended to be disrupted. This is a time to focus. This indicates that it is impermissible to interrupt the activity and resume at a later time. If an individual approaches and requests your assistance, you will be required to politely refuse or pause your session. A significant amount of work can be accomplished within a limited number of sessions.

Organize Thematic Events

The Chief Executive Officer of Square and Twitter, Mr. Jack Dorsey, dedicates eight hours daily to his enterprises. How is he productive?

He possesses a high degree of proficiency and exhibits exceptional self-control. During the commencement of each workweek at respective companies, his attention is directed toward the efficient operation and supervision of the organization. They have a directional meeting at Square and an OpCom meeting at Twitter. He engages in the day's individualized management tasks.

On Tuesdays, his primary attention is directed towards the product. On Wednesday, his focus is directed towards the areas of growth, communications, and marketing. On

Thursday, his primary focus lies in nurturing partnerships and cultivating relationships with developers, while on Friday, he dedicates his attention to recruiting efforts and fostering a positive corporate culture.

On Saturday, he hikes. Sundays are dedicated to strategic planning and self-reflection in preparation for the upcoming week. The primary factor contributing to the effectiveness of theme days is their ability to maintain his focus. In the event of an interruption, he possesses the capability to efficiently handle the issue at hand and promptly resume his previous task.

Refrain from making decisions

If you have ever pondered the reasoning behind the consistent attire choices of individuals such as

Steve Jobs, Barack Obama, and Mark Zuckerberg, it is not attributable to their lack of fashion acumen or indolence. Rather, it signifies a deliberate allocation of their cognitive resources.

As the day progresses, our capacity to make sound decisions will diminish. By refraining from making choices, we are mitigating the occurrence of a phenomenon recognized as decision fatigue.

Individuals who demonstrate high levels of productivity effectively mitigate decision fatigue through the strategic implementation of streamlining and automating various decision-making processes. One possible alternative in a formal tone could be: "This may involve arranging your attire in advance, preparing your meals on a designated day of the week, and employing software tools to coordinate and plan your meetings."

Adaptable Schedules

Implementing a systematic approach to time management will foster organization and concentration, but it is essential to strike a balance by refraining from meticulously allocating tasks to every minute of your day. Hence, individuals who are accomplished and efficient make an effort to allocate vacant time slots in their schedules. Upon incorporating scheduled activities into your available time slots, a transformation will become evident within yourself.

This encompasses the act of pausing to collect oneself, engage in introspection, or contemplate. You may harbor the notion that you lack the time to engage in idleness. One possible way to address this is to allot a buffer time of ten minutes when scheduling a meeting anticipated to run for approximately thirty minutes. By doing so, a ten-minute window will be created for you to engage in activities of your choice either prior to or subsequent to your scheduled meeting.

An alternative choice would be to leave an entire day unassigned. Tim Ferriss shall refrain from scheduling any activities on Mondays or Fridays. He instructs his assistants to refrain from answering phone calls on Mondays and Fridays, as a precautionary measure in case he wishes to extend his weekend leisure. He regularly designates Mondays for the purpose of prioritizing, preparing, and managing any administrative duties he may have to undertake.

As there are no appointments or obligations in his schedule, he has the freedom to decide how to allocate his time. All of the responsibilities are neither disagreeable nor motivated by financial considerations. In the event that he is presented with an opportunity for spontaneous enjoyment, he is capable of swiftly cancelling his prior commitments.

Unwind Every Night

Due to the fact that individuals who are highly productive lead gratifying yet demanding lifestyles, they generally allocate time for personal relaxation and leisure activities during each evening. Why? They are afforded the opportunity to rejuvenate and prepare for the ensuing day. How do they occupy their time when they are not engaged in their professional duties? They engage in activities of their own preference, thereby attaining relaxation and alleviating their stress levels. Subsequently, they make preparations for bedtime and allocate a duration of approximately six to eight hours for restful sleep.

Polyphasic Sleeping

This approach may appear unconventional and is likely to be effective for only a limited number of individuals. Should you discover that it yields favorable results for you, you will undoubtedly observe a substantial increase in productivity throughout the course of your day.

The majority of individuals adhere to a sleep pattern commonly referred to as monophasic sleep. This essentially implies that you obtain the entirety of your sleep during the nocturnal hours, typically in a continuous period lasting approximately eight hours. Individuals who engage in a sleep pattern characterized by two shorter intervals of rest, typically lasting around four hours each, during both the morning and the evening, can be classified as biphasic sleepers. Individuals who adopt polyphasic sleep patterns rigorously embrace and push the boundaries of this technique. They segment their sleep patterns into multiple phases, with reduced duration, to enhance productivity. The amount of sleep obtained during each phase may vary. Certain individuals may opt for a mere twenty-minute slumber, while others may require a more substantial duration of rest and subsequently augment it with additional naps.

A project manager of Russian nationality has recently adopted a methodology wherein he allocates a mere 3.5 hours for sleep during the night, complemented by three brief twenty-minute naps throughout the day. As a result of this circumstance, he asserts that he possesses an increased amount of working hours, consequently enabling him to accomplish a greater volume of tasks compared to his usual capacity. A key advantage he enjoys is the allocation of two months annually as leisure time, free of obligations.

Polyphasic sleep has the potential to enhance your alertness and overall well-being. It has the potential to deliver a more gratifying sleeping experience and has been shown to enhance one's productivity. This scheduling does possess certain disadvantages. Living with this particular sleep schedule poses a considerable challenge, especially when attempting to balance the demands of daily family life. If you fail to adhere to your scheduled sleep sessions, it may disrupt your equilibrium.

There are numerous benefits associated with this approach, such as the ability to effectively utilize additional working hours throughout the day. An individual who limits their sleep to a mere four hours per night will find themselves with an additional twenty-eight hours each week to allocate towards their work or other activities.

Discovering the Optimal Combination

In order to discover the optimal schedule for your maximum productivity, it may be necessary to develop a combination incorporating elements from these various options. This methodology is highly effective when utilizing the technique of time blocking. It is possible to accommodate three Pomodoro sessions within a duration of ninety minutes. It is possible that you will need to pursue the polyphasic method independently.

It is imperative that you arrange and manage your daily activities. Should you choose not to, someone else shall. By establishing a daily agenda, you will ensure that you are the one taking the lead in prioritizing your life.

What Are The Potential Benefits Of Implementing Time Management Practices In My Life?

Effective time management plays a pivotal role in fostering professional growth as well as maintaining a healthy balance in one's personal life. "Let us now explore some of the significant advantages of time management."

Effective Time Management diminishes stress levels."
The primary focus of effective time management pertains to the reduction of stress levels. If one effectively implements the principles of time management, optimal outcomes can be achieved. One can also experience a state of relaxation while engaging in their work.

Tension cables that disrupt work schedules will never yield optimal outcomes.

Effective time management enables individuals to concentrate more effectively on their tasks.
Achieving a state of profound concentration can be facilitated by prearranging your tasks prior to undertaking them, leading to enhanced outcomes and sustainable success in the long run.
Individuals consistently aspire to achieve a prosperous and pleasurable existence, which can be attained through upholding a steadfast perspective and attentively navigating each subsequent action.

Effective time management mitigates the propensity for procrastination.

The specific aspect involved in the implementation of time management pertains to the capacity to anticipate results and exert command over circumstances.

Efficient time management can be achieved by maintaining a strong sense of focus on one's objectives and refraining from making excuses that facilitate procrastination, thereby demonstrating that specialized skills are unnecessary in this regard.

Effective time management can enhance your self-assurance: Self-assurance plays a crucial role in an individual's life, and those who possess confidence tend to have more favorable experiences compared to those who rely on others.

The prevailing sentiment is that effective job planning, coupled with timely decision-making for enhancement, is crucial. Efficient time management allows individuals to effectively allocate their time, consequently providing them with additional time for various pursuits. A person's unwavering confidence, in turn, propels them towards elevated accomplishments and personal growth.

Effective time management paves the way towards achieving your objectives: The entirety of humanity aspires to accomplish one or multiple objectives in life and envisions attaining a prosperous future upon attaining said objectives.

Organizing Your Life

I intend to discuss several organizational strategies in this chapter that can greatly enhance your productivity. Maintaining a sense of organization enables individuals to efficiently manage their belongings while gaining insight into their inventory and quantities. Such meticulousness aids in both monetary savings and potential financial gains.

46. Arrange every room in your residence in a meticulous manner, ensuring that you possess a precise knowledge of the location of each and every item. This aspect holds significant importance in terms of increasing productivity. You should endeavor to avoid expending excessive time in search of the necessary resources to successfully accomplish the project at hand.

47. Maintain an ongoing inventory of the items stored within your cabinets and

shelves. If you operate a home-based enterprise specializing in crafting artisanal jewelry, it is imperative to possess precise knowledge regarding the inventory at your disposal. In the event that you are not operating a commercial enterprise from your residence, it remains imperative to possess knowledge regarding the whereabouts and quantification of each item within your premises.

48. Do not acquire excessive quantities of a particular item if you lack adequate storage space. This occurrence is a regular phenomenon in my observations. People discover remarkable bargains during their shopping excursions and consequently acquire quantities of the product that surpass their storage capacity. They resort to inventive storage solutions, placing it in any available space, only to ultimately neglect it, resulting in a regrettable misuse of their financial resources. Please ensure that you have essential items readily available, without

exceeding your immediate requirements.

49. Implementing efficient organization greatly facilitates the cleaning process at the conclusion of the day. Every individual residing in the household, including yourself, possesses the knowledge of each item's designated place, resulting in a more efficient process of retrieving and returning objects as compared to a scenario where they lack assigned spaces.

Maintaining a sense of organization should transcend the confines of your dwelling; it is imperative to foster orderliness in every facet of life, particularly with regard to the consumption of time. Ensure that you arrange and plan your days in advance, preferably the evening prior. Retrieve all the necessary items for the following day. Please endeavor to implement any feasible measures that could facilitate a more streamlined and less burdensome day for yourself tomorrow compared to the present day.

Just Do It!

It is plausible that while perusing this text, you may harbor the belief that achieving these tasks is insurmountable. You know what? As long as you persist in maintaining that mindset, the commencement of your endeavors to achieve your goals will remain elusive. This leads me to conclude with my last piece of advice.

50. Just Do It!!!

You understood correctly, no justifications will be accepted. Cease any tendency to delay tasks, avoid establishing order, and abstain from cultivating productivity in your aforementioned pursuits. This book furnishes all the essential tools necessary for transforming your life, commencing from this very day! It is my sincere aspiration that you can assimilate the entirety of the knowledge presented in this book and effectively apply it towards effecting a substantial change in your life, commencing today.

Additionally, I would like to emphasize that this process is perpetual. Once you cease your efforts in implementing the strategies outlined in this book, procrastination will promptly resurge and endeavor to regain dominance over your existence. Don't let it!

Kindly adhere to my suggestions and derive maximum benefit from them.

Optimal Timeframe For Addressing Routine Responsibilities

Electronic mail is a continuous process. The issue associated with frequent interruptions for email responses every five minutes is that it encroaches upon the time that should be allocated to engaging in more productive pursuits. Certainly, it is essential to respond to your emails within a reasonable period, but it is not necessary to repeatedly interrupt your focused work on your task list for this purpose. Individuals who engage in such behavior will discover that they significantly compromise efficiency and productivity due to their susceptibility to distractions. It is imperative that a designated period be established during which emails shall be diligently reviewed and promptly addressed.

You must acquire proficiency in effectively utilizing your email platform. If you allocate a designated timeframe for managing your electronic correspondence, you could consider configuring an automated response system to inform individuals that you will promptly attend to their messages at your earliest convenience. It is possible to periodically alter the message, a relatively simple task that can be accomplished within seconds. However, by providing a response to their inquiries, a sense of contentment can be brought to the individuals in question. The type of verbiage employed in my documents adheres to established norms, and I maintain a standardized Word document containing all the textual content. This eliminates the need for repetitive typing on each occasion.

I express my gratitude for the email you have sent. Kindly be advised that I am presently occupied at the moment; however, I will promptly revert to you in the near future.

This is a common approach, but you have the option to enhance it or provide additional specificity by designating a specific time of day for responding to emails.

I sincerely appreciate your email. I conduct a daily review of my email correspondence at approximately 10 a.m., at which time I shall provide a response to your message. If, in the interim, this matter is of an urgent nature, please feel free to reach out to me by using my cellular phone number.

The intention behind these notes is to ensure that your clients are informed of the receipt of their email. Next, you must determine how to allocate time throughout your day to address emails without any form of interruption, thereby enabling you to promptly process them and attain an empty inbox. Please bear in mind that engaging in multitasking will not prove beneficial when you are confronted with multiple tasks that demand completion. Consequently, allocate thirty minutes on two occasions throughout the day specifically for addressing emails. A suitable alternative in a formal tone would be: "This could occur upon your initial arrival at the office in the morning, as well as upon your return from the midday meal break."

Subsequently, carefully review the emails and assess their degree of urgency. Several of these inquiries will be easily addressable without significant contemplation, which will effectively reduce the number of emails requiring your attention once they have been resolved. Subsequently, attend to those matters for which you possess sufficient knowledge and resourcefulness, thereby obviating the need to physically retrieve additional information from outside your workspace. In conclusion, address the lengthy emails or those that may necessitate additional research prior to providing a response. It is essential to establish a highly efficient email filing system to ensure prompt access to necessary information. It is not advisable to sift through 5000 emails in an attempt to locate the specific one that provides the necessary information. If you categorize and arrange them into distinct containers, you will have the advantage of knowing their specific locations, thus significantly economizing on your time.

In order to expedite your efficiency, there are specific measures that can be taken. As an illustration, the salutation utilized at the beginning of the email is nearly customary. By maintaining a record of the content you frequently communicate, you can compile a collection of standardized email templates. This enables you to easily incorporate the appropriate template into your email response if you utilize a Customer Relationship Management (CRM) system or similar email management platform. In the absence of a CRM, it is advisable to maintain a distinct file containing all relevant information. However, it is imperative to configure your email settings in a manner such that your professional signature is preloaded. This will facilitate significant time savings.

If you establish a systematic approach and maintain good organizational practices, the completion of routine bulk tasks should not demand a significant amount of your time. "If you are unable to provide a solution to a problem encountered in a business setting, it is advisable to refrain from responding to the individual and conveying the message:

I am not sure. I will need to investigate the matter and provide you with a response later.

It does not exhibit the utmost professionalism. It would be highly preferable if you could direct the client's query to a colleague who possesses the necessary expertise and consequently respond to the client in the following manner:

Your email has been forwarded to my colleague, ………. ……, who will promptly respond and address your inquiry. Allow me to provide you with the pertinent information: his email address is ……………………………..

By accomplishing this task, you are effectively removing it from your list of pending duties, or in fact, it will never become an item on your agenda. Your colleague can assume responsibility and your task is completed regarding this matter, without any outstanding issues remaining.

That approach demonstrates a higher level of practicality in handling email, thereby ensuring optimization of time and reduction of wasted efforts on unresolved matters. There is a significant amount of time squandered in the process of searching for answers. Once you commence the task of addressing your emails, proceed to respond to them accordingly. Please refrain from engaging in conversations on instant messaging platforms. Do not postpone any of them for a later time, as the future is uncertain. Additionally, ensure that your automatic responses are configured to endure until you resume attending to emails from your designated work area.

This provides a significant sense of tranquility as it assures you that all incoming matters have been addressed, allowing you to ensure that anyone who contacts you after the session will receive a response, even if it is simply to inform them of a pending reply. It is preferable to receive any form of acknowledgement rather than none, as it endeavors to maintain the satisfaction of all parties involved.

Alternative duties

Email management should not be regarded as the sole routine obligation, and effectively categorizing your correspondence into prioritized stacks can be of assistance. When managing paperwork, it is advisable to organize it into distinct categories, namely the pile that can be efficiently handled, the one that necessitates collaboration with others, and the one that demands immediate attention. Prioritize the pressing matters at the beginning of the day, and subsequently, if there is a surplus of time after addressing your email correspondence, devote your attention to the abundance of tasks that are simpler to handle in order to effectively streamline your workload. If there are any documents or communications that require additional input from others, consider utilizing the camera functionality on your mobile device to capture them and subsequently share them with the respective individuals. That takes seconds. You can also mark it to say that you did that and follow up later on. In this manner, what remains is solely the matter that genuinely necessitates your attention and can be efficiently managed while you are in a state of high energy. Therefore, following a pause or subsequent to your meal would be the opportune moment. By the conclusion of the day, it is expected that all of your paperwork and emails will have been attended to, thus ensuring that your work surface is uncluttered and prepared for the next morning. Any pending tasks that remain unaddressed should be promptly scheduled and accompanied by a reminder on your calendar, allowing for their seamless integration into your agenda for the subsequent day.

Distraction is the diversion that draws your focus away from the task at hand. If one is incessantly compelled to frequently inspect their email, that particular diversion would impede the successful completion of academic tasks.

A diversion can alternatively serve as a respite for relaxation. If you have concerns regarding your impending dance performance tomorrow, viewing a nonsensical action film might serve as a gratifying diversion that aids in your relaxation.

Has it ever been brought to your attention that your behavior is causing me significant frustration and exasperation? When one becomes exceedingly preoccupied, their state of agitation can be so profound that it induces a sense of mental instability. Distraction pertains to the state of being diverted from the intended focus of a task or preoccupations.

Effective Techniques for Eliminating Distractions and Enhancing Concentration

You currently reside in a smaller urban center, situated within the outskirts of a major metropolitan area. On a clear day, during the middle of the week, when one desires to embark on a journey to an alternate city (city B).

The most expeditious and optimal approach to arrive at city B would be by selecting the street route. It may require some time for you to reach your destination, considering your residence in downtown. However, once you achieve it, you will promptly find yourself in B. Now envision a scenario where, due to unforeseen circumstances, the thoroughfare is inaccessible, prompting you to opt for privately-owned routes or thoroughfares.

At first, it may appear more expeditious as there is no need to traverse the entire street, allowing you to commence your journey towards B immediately upon departing from your residence. Nevertheless, once one embarks on their journey, they quickly comprehend the prevalence of numerous traffic lights and stop signs along the side streets. Frequent interruptions necessitate numerous stops, thus resulting in a doubling of the duration of your journey.

One begins to yearn for the opportunity to have traversed the street.

The presence of stop signs and traffic lights would impede your journey, while distractions would impair your productivity and concentration. Engaging in tasks while consistently experiencing interruptions from a myriad of sources can significantly enhance the efficiency with which the task is accomplished.

It has been established through a range of studies that seemingly innocuous minor distractions necessitate an average of 21 minutes for one to regain their focus and concentration. Without a doubt, distractions continue to remain a significant detriment to productivity.

Let us embark on the path of enhancing productivity and meticulously examine the most effective, extensively tested approaches for their eradication.

Kill instantaneous notifications

Notifications across various applications utilized for communication are among the most significant sources of distraction.

Terminate the Skype application (or activate the Do Not Disturb mode), close all email clients, log out from social networking platforms, as well as disable other chat applications.

If you are in need of guidance pertaining to the task at hand, it would be advisable to seek assistance and refrain from any communication activities while working.

Please ensure that the telephone is relocated.

Please set your mobile phone to vibrate mode or silence it. Preferably, relocate it to an alternative location. Majority of smartphones possess considerable vibrational strength, and their vibrations can be audibly detected when they are in close proximity to you. Hence, it is advised to position them at the maximum feasible distance.

What if I were to overlook a significant phone call or message? You might be of the opinion.

Chances are high that you will never.

If one engages in continuous operation for 50 minutes, immediately accompanied by a brief pause lasting 5 to 10 seconds, this would be an ideal approach to segment one's time. Furthermore, it is permissible to consult one's mobile device during these interludes.

Additionally, it is advisable to arrange a specific time slot in your daily schedule for making and receiving phone calls. It is conceivable to compile your voicemail to disclose this information. When an individual contacts you within the agreed-upon timeframe, they will have a clear expectation of when to anticipate your response.

By employing this approach, you can ensure that your focus remains undisturbed during task execution, simultaneously ensuring that others do not feel disgruntled by their inability to establish communication with you.

Terminate all unnecessary applications

If you are operating a personal computer, it is advisable to keep only the necessary applications open that are required for the particular task at hand.

If you are engaged in writing, it is advisable to have access to a word processor. Consider adopting a "full-screen" writing approach to minimize distractions significantly.

If you desire to utilize an internet browser, it would be advisable to maintain only a solitary tab open.

If you do not need internet access, consider disconnecting the cable or disabling the wireless connection. This has the potential to mitigate a considerable number of diversions. A minor caveat is that, depending on the applications you have installed, a few of them might generate notifications indicating their unsuccessful attempts to establish a connection with the internet.

In alternative terms, the act of not staying connected could potentially create more disturbances than the act of staying connected. This is a matter deserving careful scrutiny.

Launch all necessary applications

It is imperative that all requisite documents and software programs be opened prior to commencing the assigned task. There is a likelihood that you may become diverted while attempting to locate the specific document amidst your notes for your task, or while seeking the shortcut that launches the additional software you desire.

Precede your tasks with a moment of reflection and organization. This will enable you to gather your thoughts, ascertain the essential documentation and applications required for completing the business.

"Educate" additional people

Many of the interruptions and distractions in life arise from the individuals in your vicinity. Whether they are colleagues, significant others, family members, acquaintances, or even domestic animals.

The optimal strategy to prevent such occurrences would involve establishing a set of guidelines and effectively communicating them to all individuals involved. Kindly communicate your preference to work in concentrated intervals and express your appreciation if they could limit any interruptions, thus allowing you to maintain focus and productivity during these specified periods.

Additionally, it would facilitate comprehension to affirm that it is imperative for you to dedicate your full attention to both parties during each break, as opposed to allocating them a meager fraction (or less) in the event that they disrupt your current activities.

Familiarize yourself with your Do Not Disturb (DND) indicator.

This will provide notification to individuals of your current focused state and indicate whether it is permissible to approach you for conversation. The DND signal can be used to indicate that one should not be disturbed while at work, if such a signal is present. In that case, it is advisable to wear headphones or utilize any other suitable means of establishing personal focus. Ensure that you effectively convey the importance of the gesture to the outside world.

Please refrain from any improper use of the Do Not Disturb (DND) feature by continuously enabling it. This can create the perception of constant engagement (despite clear signs to the contrary), thereby diminishing the respect accorded to it. Please position it prominently when it is of utmost importance to capture your attention, ensuring however that you subsequently remove it to indicate your willingness to address the concerns of others.

If you decide to work from home, it is advisable to consider disabling the doorbell in order to minimize distractions caused by neighbors, mail deliveries, or unexpected visitors soliciting donations or trying to sell goods.

Use headphones

Frequently, it is desirable to function in a conducive setting. Transitioning from the ambience of the outdoors, characterized by construction and traffic noises, to the cacophony generated by intrusive neighbors and talkative colleagues, certain sounds can prove to be remarkably disruptive.

An excellent approach would involve utilizing headphones to enjoy musical compositions. If you find music to be more of a source of distraction, consider utilizing headphones primarily for noise isolation purposes or playing ambient white noise in order to counterbalance any potential distractions.

Headphones serve as a highly effective indication of one's unavailability, thus enabling the accomplishment of two objectives simultaneously.

Clear visual clutter

Please ensure that you tidy your table, paying particular attention to your notes.

Do not portray the individual:" "Do not assume the role of the person:" "Do not personify the individual:" "Do not embody the person:

distractions

Remove any objects or materials within your immediate surroundings that may serve as distractions, deliberately diverting your attention away from an activity or task.

Clear PC Clutter

Please undertake the cleaning of your electronic desk in the same manner that you washed your physical desk, with equal precision and thoroughness.

Please clear your desktop computer or remove any additional documents, programs, and shortcuts from the display.

When utilizing a web browser for professional purposes, it is advisable to employ an ad blocker to eliminate all banner ads, pop-ups, and other intrusive advertisements that have the potential to divert your attention.

Ensure proper maintenance of physical necessities.

Ensure that you have a bottle of your preferred beverage readily available in close proximity. Please take into consideration the inclusion of a snack as well. It can prove to be rather distracting to have to arise and relocate to another area in order to procure a beverage, thus it is best to be prepared.

Utilize your break periods to visit the lavatory in order to minimize the need to divide your focus for nature's calls.

Fix room temperature

If you have the ability to adjust the ambient temperature, it is recommended to set it to a comfortable level conducive to optimal productivity, such as 25 degrees Celsius or 77 degrees Fahrenheit.

If you find yourself working in a traditional office setting or in settings such as a local coffee shop, library, or any place where temperature regulation is not possible, it is advisable to make necessary preparations. Having additional garments readily available.

If you have a designated area, such as a cubicle, it would be advisable to consider acquiring a compact fan for excessively warm and humid days, as well as a small heater for excessively cold and freezing ones. All of these factors can prevent you from having to divide your attention in order to accomplish the process of heating up or cooling down.

Please turn off your clock.

Maintaining constant awareness of the precise time can prove to be a noteworthy source of diversion. Especially when faced with limited time, witnessing the rapid passage of moments can cause significant stress as well.

Removing the element of time from the equation will enable you to direct your attention towards the completion of the task, rather than fixating on its duration.

Conceal the time display on your personal computer, place your mobile phone out of sight, remove your wristwatch, and eradicate any wall or alarm clocks positioned on the walls or shelves surrounding you. It is an emancipating sensation to be free of concerns regarding the constraints of time.

To ensure that you do not miss any important meetings or time-sensitive events, it is advised to set up a reminder on your computer or mobile device.

Exceeding your current level

Distractions can significantly hinder productivity, hence it is crucial to adopt a proactive approach and make concerted efforts to minimize their impact. It necessitates a modest investment of time and preparation in order to effectively manage one's surroundings for optimal levels of attention. Nevertheless, the advantages in terms of productivity are indeed valuable. Ultimately, opting for major thoroughfares is invariably more favorable when juxtaposed with navigating through local roadways.

The Procrastination-Action Line

Procrastination can be seen as the application of brakes, while taking action can be regarded as the release of those brakes.

Upon crossing the Action Line, the onset of pain alleviation becomes evident. The experience of being caught in a state of procrastination can be considerably more distressing than being actively engaged in completing the work. The internal anguish encompassed by guilt, shame, and anxiety during periods of procrastination typically surpasses the exertion and vigor required during the work process. The issue does not reside in executing the task, but rather in initiating the task.

In order to cease the act of procrastination, it is imperative that we simplify the process for the Present Self to initiate tasks, while maintaining faith that motivation and momentum will manifest once the commencement is made. Momentum frequently materializes subsequent to initiation, rather than preceding it.

There exist numerous approaches that we can utilize in order to cease the habit of procrastination. The following elucidates and provides a comprehensive description of each concept, subsequently accompanied by illustrative instances showcasing the implementation of strategy.

Alternative: "Proposal 1: Enhance the Timeliness of Incentives for Encouraging Action"

If one can devise strategies to render the advantages of long-term decisions more promptly attainable, the likelihood of succumbing to procrastination diminishes.

For instance: You take great pleasure in indulging in lavish expenditures. You have received guidance from a person who wishes you well, suggesting the initiation of a Systematic Investment Plan in reputable debt mutual funds, with the aim of accumulating a significant amount for your future. Somehow, you have exhibited a tendency to engage in procrastination regarding this matter due to a lack of enthusiasm towards the monetary value that would be bestowed upon you after a period of 25 years.

However, when the investment advisor or mutual fund manager provides you with the monthly or quarterly report on your current assets, you are able to gain awareness of the incremental value of your assets and experience a sense of increased financial abundance. This will induce you to allocate funds towards additional Systematic Investment Plans (SIPs).

Alternative 2: Encouragement Cohesion:

A strategy recognized as temptation bundling is an effective means to integrate forthcoming benefits with the present moment.

The notion of temptation bundling emerged as a result of research conducted by Katy Milkman at The University of Pennsylvania within the field of behavioral economics. In essence, the strategy proposes the combination of a behavior that yields long-term benefits with a behavior that provides immediate gratification.

The fundamental structure entails combining the activities that bring you joy with the tasks that you typically find yourself inclined to defer.

"Presented below are several prevalent instances of temptation bundling:

You have consistently delayed engaging in physical activity. You derive immense pleasure from indulging in audiobooks pertaining to your selected subject matter.

There is the option to combine the two activities and arrange to listen to your preferred audiobook solely during your exercise session. Engage exclusively with audiobooks or podcasts that you have a genuine affinity for when engaging in physical activity.

Alternative Option 3: Implement Measures to Prompt More Immediate Consequences of Procrastination

There exist numerous methods to expedite your accountability for the consequences of delaying action, sooner rather than later. For instance, in the event that you are engaging in physical activity in solitary, refraining from your workout during the upcoming week will have minimal influence upon your daily life. Your physical well-being will not immediately decline as a result of skipping a single workout. The consequences of postponing physical activity only manifest in discomfort and inconvenience after extended periods of inactivity. Nevertheless, should you make a serious commitment to engage in physical exercise with a companion at 7 a.m. on the upcoming Monday, the consequence of skipping your routine becomes more promptly apparent. If you happen to skip this particular exercise session, your acquaintance might refer to you as discourteous.

An additional prevailing method entails the imposition of a sanction upon your person. Failure to follow through on your commitments may result in your acquaintances taking advantage of your generosity. The purpose of this notion is to establish an alternative outcome that occurs in the event of failure to promptly engage in the specified behavior.

Alternative 4: Enhance Feasibility of the Task

As previously discussed, the primary source of procrastination lies in the inhibition to initiate a particular behavior. Upon commencement, the act of consistently persevering tends to alleviate the degree of discomfort experienced. This serves as a compelling rationale for minimizing the magnitude of your routines, as cultivating smaller and more manageable habits not only facilitates their initiation but also mitigates the tendency to succumb to procrastination.

An effective strategy I employ to facilitate the adoption of new habits involves implementing the 2-Minute Rule. This principle posits that when embarking on a new habit, the initial action required should be feasible within a two-minute timeframe. The rationale behind this approach is to minimize obstacles to initiation and bank on the subsequent momentum to propel one further into the task once it has commenced. Once an individual initiates an action, it becomes more convenient to sustain its execution. The 2–Minute Rule effectively addresses the issues of procrastination and idleness by presenting such a simple and effortless way to initiate action that one cannot refuse.

An additional effective approach to render tasks more attainable is to disaggregate them. As an illustration, let us contemplate the exceptional level of productivity demonstrated by the renowned wordsmith, Anthony Trollope. He has authored a total of 47 novels, 18 pieces of non-fiction literature, 12 short stories, 2 plays, and an array of articles and letters. What was the method employed by him to accomplish this task? Rather than evaluating his progress in terms of finished chapters or books, Trollope gauged his progress by dividing it into intervals of 15 minutes. He established a target of producing 250 words within a 15-minute interval, and diligently adhered to this regimen for a duration of three hours daily. This methodology enabled him to experience sentiments of gratification and achievement at regular intervals, all the while persevering with the substantial undertaking of composing a book.

It is of utmost significance to ensure that your tasks are rendered more feasible for two primary reasons.

Incremental advancements contribute to the sustenance of momentum in the long term, thereby increasing the probability of successfully completing substantial undertakings.

The more expediently you accomplish a task that yields productivity, the more swiftly your day assumes an ambiance characterized by productivity and efficacy.

Technique 12 - Conquer Procrastination

Without a doubt, procrastination is the time-wasting habit that plagues everyone. One can scarcely fathom the extent to which postponing crucial tasks exacts a toll, be it in terms of time, finances, standards, or the well-being of individuals. It is prudent to consistently bear in mind the immutable truth that time is unforgiving, and there can be no justification for protracting the execution of tasks that hold paramount significance and urgency in one's life.

Perfectionism is a contributing factor that hinders the completion of a task. Individuals often anticipate an opportune moment to undertake a particular action, despite the absence of such an optimal occasion. Nonetheless, this does not imply that you will compromise on the aspect of quality in exchange for timeliness. Instead, it pertains to initiating despite not feeling like the primary individual.

One additional factor contributing to procrastination is the inclination to seek distractions, particularly following the completion of a task. It is their conviction that they are entitled to a respite; however, it transpires that following a mere 20 minutes of labor, they proceed to engage in 2 hours of video game recreation. Adhering to a predetermined timetable can assist in overcoming this condition.

The most effective approach in overcoming procrastination is to readily embark upon the initial task. For example, in the event that you have the need to compose an essay, it would be prudent to commence the process by developing a comprehensive outline. This will serve as a source of inspiration to encourage perseverance rather than succumbing to inaction.

Skill 13 - Engage in Proactive Self-Motivation

The ability to adhere to the predetermined schedule necessitates a sense of drive and determination. There exist two primary forms of motivation, commonly referred to as positive reinforcement and negative reinforcement.

When confronted with a daunting task, such as the completion of a report for your employer within a designated timeframe, you have the ability to inspire and propel yourself forward by contemplating the subsequent benefits that will arise upon successful completion of said task. As an illustration, should you complete the report in advance, you will have ample opportunity to refine it and incorporate further depth. Through the consistent production of exceptional work within designated timelines, your superior will undoubtedly acknowledge your intrinsic worth and be compelled to initiate your advancement or facilitate a salary increase. This serves as the incentive for progress.

In contrast, there are individuals who experience heightened motivation when they contemplate the potential repercussions of failing to complete a given task within the designated timeframe. Suppose you were to envision a situation in which you were unable to meet the deadline for submitting the report. It is likely that the outcome of your report presentation will result in profound personal embarrassment, potentially jeopardizing your professional standing and running the risk of unfavorable employment consequences. This constitutes as the tool of motivation.

Therefore, whenever you feel reluctance towards undertaking the task and delay it for a later time, it is prudent to contemplate both the potential rewards and consequences associated with each scenario.

Effective Techniques For Time Management: Unveiling The Power Of Small And Large Strategies

Time management is a prevalent challenge encountered by individuals worldwide, leading experts to diligently devise various systems aimed at resolving this issue. Presented herein are techniques that are currently highly favored and have been proposed by esteemed intellectuals.

Pomodoro Technique
We have previously discussed this matter in a prior chapter; however, it is important to note that the Pomodoro Technique, as formulated by Francesco Cirillo, is characterized by a greater degree of strictness. In accordance with this methodology, there exists a prescribed duration for exertion followed by a designated interval of relaxation. Therefore, it is not necessary to adhere to the 60:15 ratios, which stipulate working for one hour and

resting for 15 minutes for each hour worked immediately thereafter. On the contrary, the Pomodoro Technique necessitates a mere duration of 25 minutes. Presented below are the customary guidelines:

Establish your preferred assignment

Please adjust the timer to a duration of 25 minutes.

Continue working until you perceive the sound of the timer.

Upon the sounding of the timer, please indulge in a brief 5-minute respite.

Please reset the timer for another duration of 25 minutes and commence your work once more.

After completing a succession of four 25-minute sessions, equaling a total of one hour, you are entitled to a 30 minute interval.

Eisenhower Method

It has been conveyed that this approach was employed by the esteemed US President Eisenhower himself, originating from his statement, "I encounter two types of predicaments:

those that are pressing and those that are significant." In the realm of priorities, the matters that require immediate attention often do not hold significant importance, while the matters holding significant importance generally do not demand immediate attention."

"In essence, there are four boxes present, each labeled:

Urgent and Important

Non-critical yet significant

Of low priority and insignificance.

Pressing but of little significance

Afterwards, you proceed to assign tasks according to these qualifications. After completing this task, you will gain an enhanced understanding of your priorities. As a result, prioritization is given to the Urgent/Important tasks, with Urgent/Not Important tasks following thereafter.

Partner System

A partner system operates in a similar manner to the Commitment System, whereby you enlist the assistance of an individual to ensure the successful execution of your designated tasks. In contrast, within the Partner System, the functionality operates bidirectionally. You provide a gentle nudge to a companion regarding their responsibilities, and in turn, your companion reciprocates by reminding you of your own obligations. It resembles the concept of the Buddy System when it comes to weight loss. One of the benefits of this approach is that it provides an external motivation to complete tasks. However, one must acknowledge the limitation that it is not universally applicable. The Partner System can be employed for weight loss purposes; however, it may not yield the same level of effectiveness when utilized for dishwashing.

Keep It Entertaining
Creating task lists and adhering to a structured timetable can become monotonous, even when employing technological aids. Therefore, it is incumbent upon you to inject some

amusement into the task. As an illustration, should your preference entail employing post-it notes as a means of task management, an alternative method worth considering would be the adoption of a color-coded system. For instance, red could signify matters of urgency, blue could indicate items of significance, and green could represent tasks that possess a degree of flexibility in terms of postponement. One can enhance the implementation of the Eisenhower method by incorporating color coding, wherein each quadrant is designated a distinct color. Generate strategies to enhance enjoyment while effectively organizing your schedule.

Getting Things Done
This technique, abbreviated as GTD, was devised by David Allen and advocates the segmentation of tasks into manageable increments. The objective of GTD is to mitigate information overload, or more precisely, the sensation of being excessively burdened, which was deliberated upon in a earlier section.

The GTD system demonstrates greater precision by emphasizing the completion of smaller tasks as a priority. After completion, it is possible to further subdivide the major task into smaller components until its entirety is realized.

Don't Overload Yourself
Primarily, it is imperative that you do not succumb to an excessive workload. This is in regards to tasks that you have the ability to circumvent. For instance, if a colleague were to request assistance and you find it impossible to accommodate their request within your pre-existing commitments and obligations. Acquire the skill of politely declining requests from your acquaintance in order to prevent further complexity in your already intricate schedule. Please be aware that we are discussing tasks which can be completely eliminated as opposed to those which can only be postponed.

Use the Weekends

Many individuals experience a decrease in productivity due to the misconception that weekdays are exclusively meant for work and weekends for leisure. While it is important to allow yourself some leisure time, it is equally crucial to remember that the duration of Saturday and Sunday amounts to a total of 48 hours. What significance does allocating one to two hours per day for supplementary tasks hold? You will discover that allocating a small portion of your time during those hours can significantly impact your work approach on Monday, in contrast to having a complete lack of productivity.

POSEC Method

The POSEC Method, an additional remarkable approach, is gradually garnering recognition within diverse spheres. It embodies a more comprehensive methodology and represents the principles of "Prioritizing through Organization, Streamlining, Economizing, and Contribution."

Allow me to elucidate the process:

Setting priorities entails establishing the tasks or responsibilities that must be given precedence in one's life. At this juncture, you ascertain your life objectives in order to discern precisely how each day contributes.

Coordinate - effectively structure the duties that are required to be completed on a recurring basis. Simultaneously, it is advisable to compile a roster arranged in descending order of priority, ranging from the utmost significance to the comparatively less crucial. At this juncture, you may also arrange based on whether they constitute overriding concerns for professional commitments, personal matters, or familial obligations.

Optimize - this pertains to tasks that are necessary to be performed in daily life, albeit being unpleasant or undesirable. Some evident activities would include undertaking household tasks, engaging in physical exercise, and even performing specific job duties.

Practice frugality - these actions pertain to matters that lack immediacy. You have the option to complete them either today or next week, as the specific date holds little significance and will not greatly impact your life.

Contribute - this is the phase where you diligently focus on factors that have a meaningful impact on your life. It may encompass familial, friendly, philanthropic, and other communal responsibilities.

Drawing upon Maslow's Hierarchy of Needs theory, it can be posited that the POSEC Method does not function as a mere mundane strategy for Time Management, but instead serves as a comprehensive approach towards life. It is intended to assist individuals in attaining their long-term objectives by establishing a systematic framework that effectively supports the pursuit of the ultimate goal.

Utilize idle time effectively.

There are ample periods of leisure or idleness that exist within an individual's lifetime, albeit perhaps not readily discerned by most. For instance, one may devote approximately 5 minutes queuing at the grocery store, 10 minutes at the bank, 5 minutes at the filling station, and an additional 30 minutes commuting on the bus. When all of these periods of inactivity are combined, a substantial number of hours are being expended without achieving any meaningful output. On the contrary, it is advisable to consistently carry an item that can positively contribute to the accomplishment of a task. Are you required to compose a formal document? Please ensure that you have your smartphone with you and utilize it to peruse the reference materials pertaining to the report, while waiting for the doctor.

Exercise Caution Regarding the Expenditure of Your Time

You may be astonished by the extent to which you are squandering your time on non-essential activities. It is possible that you are unaware of the cumulative time you dedicate to perusing Facebook, Twitter, and other online platforms. Fortunately, in modern times, technological advancements have given rise to applications that facilitate the measurement and analysis of unproductive time spent on these social media platforms. Employing these strategies will provide you with a fresh perspective and, ideally, instigate a proactive transformation in your habitual tendency to procrastinate.

Maintaining Consistency – The Utmost Priority

The most challenging aspect of Time Management is executing tasks to completion. Typically, this is the stage at which individuals encounter difficulties, as despite having meticulously outlined, organized, and resolved to adhere to their plans, they ultimately deviate from them. On what occasion did you most recently rise promptly upon the sound of your alarm clock rather than engaging the snooze function?

Self-imposed regulations are seldom adhered to – therefore, it would be prudent to have an external party serve as a designated supervisor. This individual embodies the role of providing strong motivation and support to ensure you fulfill any obligations you have undertaken.

Naturally, not everyone is fortunate enough to possess a confidant responsible for scrutinizing their actions. "In situations of this nature, it is imperative to demonstrate the determination and resolve to execute the plans one has set for oneself." An alternative approach would be to establish an incentive program, commonly known as a reward-penalty system, to assist your progress. While this approach may not be as potent in its efficacy, it will, at the very least, initiate the process of getting you on track.

It varies among individuals.

Ultimately, it is worth noting that Time Management Systems that are effective for one individual may not necessarily be effective for others, and vice versa. While some individuals may exhibit favorable results in utilizing Time Management apps, you might discover that you perform more effectively by embracing the conventional method of using a pen and paper. The possibilities, hence, are limitless and your primary objective should be to persist in discovering an approach that resonates most effectively with your individuality.

After discovering the approach that is most effective for your needs, the subsequent tasks should become less challenging.

www.ingramcontent.com/pod-product-compliance
Lightning Source LLC
Chambersburg PA
CBHW050232120526
44590CB00016B/2058